PARANORMAL PHENOMENA

SCIENCE

AND LIFE AFTER DEATH

C0-AVH-173

E.T.S.U. AT TEXARKANA LIBRARY

~~019964~~

023830

Biographical Note

CURT JOHN DUCASSE, Professor of Philosophy Emeritus, Brown University, has had a distinguished career as teacher, lecturer, writer. He has served as president of the American Association for Symbolic Logic, the American Philosophical Association (Eastern Division), the American Society for Aesthetics, and the Philosophy of Science Association. He is a Fellow of the American Academy of Arts and Sciences.

Dr. Ducasse is interested in all aspects of parapsychology and is a member of the Board of Trustees of the American Society for Psychical Research. He is particularly concerned with precognition, physical phenomena, mediumship, and survival, and with attempts to formulate a theory or theories that would account for the occurrence of paranormal phenomena.

He has written extensively in the fields of philosophy, art, and parapsychology. One of his best known works in parapsychology is A Critical Examination of the Belief in a Life after Death *(1961).*

Paranormal Phenomena
Science
And Life After Death

C. J. Ducasse

Professor of Philosophy Emeritus
Brown University

Parapsychology Foundation, Inc.
29 West 57th Street, New York City 10019

Copyright © 1969, by Parapsychology Foundation, Inc.

All Rights Reserved

Library of Congress Catalog Card Number: 79-762-82

Manufactured in the United States of America

FOREWORD

The central function of this monograph is to put in print a lecture I first gave at Vassar in 1962, and subsequently repeated at some five other colleges or universities, the topic of which, *Paranormal Phenomena, Science, and Life After Death,* turned out to be of such wide interest that in each case audiences much larger than had been expected and planned for showed up. This seems a good reason to make the lecture available in print, enduringly.

C. J. DUCASSE

Editor's Note: This lecture and the following two related papers were written separately and at different times; therefore, a certain amount of repetition is unavoidable.

CONTENTS

019964

0238306

INTRODUCTION

The three papers that I have the pleasure of introducing are philosophical pieces of wide public interest. On the subject of public interest in philosophy Bertrand Russell[1] observes that "during the last hundred and sixty years or so philosophy has come to be regarded as almost as technical as mathematics." Russell thinks this is unfortunate because in fact "[p]hilosophy . . . deals with matters of interest to the general educated public, and loses much of its value if only a few professionals can understand what is said." Descartes, Leibniz, Locke, Berkeley, and Hume, he says, addressed themselves not only to other philosophers "but to that much larger public which is interested in philosophical questions without being willing or able to devote more than a limited amount of time to considering them."

Among contemporary philosophers who have addressed much of their professional work to the larger public of which Russell speaks, two of the most distinguished are Russell himself and C. J. Ducasse. Like Russell's own, moreover, Ducasse's work is characterized by a rare combination of versatility, lucidity, and insight. The range of his inquiries is prodigious. Epistemology, metaphysics, ethics, aesthetics, philosophical method, philosophy of religion, and philosophy of science (including parapsychology): these are the areas with which he has been concerned. They cover most of philosophy, to whose progress and profit Ducasse has devoted most of his life. Born in France in 1881, and now Professor Emeritus of Philosophy at Brown University, the institution with which he has been continuously associated in various teaching and administrative capacities since 1926, Ducasse is still, in his eighty-eighth year, characteristically and productively engaged in the business of philosophizing for philosophers and others.[2]

To Russell's "general educated public" there are likely few subjects in philosophy of more interest than the question of personal survival of bodily death, yet in contemporary philosophy it is widely ignored. Philosophers write whole books on the concept of mind without even mentioning it. And usually when it is referred to, what is said has hardly more force than a footnote. Indeed, a list of the solid and stimulating contributions to the problem in recent philosophy would perforce be short, but it would show that a large share of the included works bear the authorship of C. J. Ducasse. For in his view, philosophical treatment of minds and persons cannot properly confine itself to the analysis of mind as exhibited biologically but must attempt as well an assessment of the possibility that mind exists also in a discarnate state.

The papers that follow, originally presented in 1958 and 1962, are fine examples of Ducasse's philosophical interest in the problem of survival. This interest had received its first major expression some years earlier in the Agnes E. and Constantine E. A. Foerster Lecture on the Immortality of the Soul delivered by Ducasse at the University of California in 1947 and entitled "Is a life after death possible?" In this lecture, which set the stage for much of his later work in the area and which I shall now briefly outline, Ducasse tries to clarify just what we are asking when we inquire into the possibility of a life after death. He states at the outset that most men crave a continuation of conscious individual existence after the death of their bodies and then proceeds to examine a number of arguments which are sometimes thought to show that such a continuation is impossible. These arguments turn largely on the alleged complete causal dependence of mental events on physical ones or, alternatively, on the contention that conscious states are really themselves nothing but physico-chemical events occurring in the nervous system or that consciousness is to be defined in terms of certain types of behavior. Whether Ducasse is right in holding that *most* men crave personal survival—my own impression is that he isn't—he succeeds, I think, in showing that the examined arguments are inconclusive and that, for all we know, "some forms of consciousness may exist independently of connection with animal or human bodies. . . ."[3]

The lecture invites us to view the problem "in cosmic rather than myopic perspective," where it is a mark of myopia, we may infer, to proceed on the tacit assumption "that *to be real is to be material*" (p. 14). This assumption, Ducasse says, while "useful and

[10]

appropriate . . . for the purpose of investigating [and operating upon] the material world," becomes useless and incongruous when not related to that specific purpose and when in particular it is carried over to investigations of mind, where it is apt, for example, to misguide us into thinking that "weak arguments against the possibility of survival . . . [are] strong" (pp. 14, 15). He offers a different, and in his view fairer, perspective, in which the relation between body and mind can be observed without prejudice as to whether the latter can exist without the former. He considers briefly some of the findings of psychical research that are *prima facie* suggestive of survival (findings that are set forth more abundantly in the present papers) and concludes by outlining some of the forms that post-mortal survival might take, if it occurs at all. Of these forms he finds reincarnation to be the most plausible, as well as being "the conception of survival probably most widespread among the peoples of the earth" (p. 30).

Supposing reincarnation to occur, what is it that might be reincarnated? In the Foerster lecture the beginnings of an answer are given in terms of a distinction between a man's *personality* and his *individuality*. The former "consists of everything he has acquired since birth: habits, skills, memories, and so on" (p. 26). The latter "comprises the aptitudes and dispositions which are native in him . . . simple ones, such as aptitude for tweezer dexterity . . . [and] others more elusive: intellectual, social, and aesthetic aptitudes, dispositions, and types of interest or of taste" (p. 26). And Ducasse speculates that it would be this inborn, native part of a human being's mind that would be reborn should metempsychosis be a fact—"the core of positive and negative capacities and tendencies that we have called a man's individuality . . . the fact might further be," he adds, "that, perhaps as a result of persistent striving to acquire a skill or trait he desires, but for which he now has little gift, aptitude for it in further births would be generated and incorporated into his individuality" (p. 27).

Now unlike Ducasse I do not myself see that reincarnation is intrinsically more plausible than any of the other forms of survival considered by him. It might be thought, indeed, that difficulties about memory, or rather the evident lack of it, render it somewhat *less* plausible than the other forms, but in the light of what Ducasse

[11]

says this appears not to be so. While the problem of memory remains a source of philosophical controversy in connection with the reincarnation view and likely a source of extra-philosophical misgivings as well, Ducasse tends to show that from a theoretical or logical standpoint it is not a major stumbling-block. For he points out in effect that we do not necessarily have to remember a previous life in order to have lived it. Suppose that a man's individuality is successively incarnated in a number of bodies, say . . . D, E, F, . . .: it is possible, for example, that in the period between the death of D and the birth of E he remembers some of his D-life experiences, but that these are all forgotten in the process of being reborn as E. It is further possible that in the interval between his E and F embodiments he remembers nothing of his E-life experiences at all. Some of these, however, could be recollected by him subsequently, during his F-life, in which case, perhaps, we should have a situation like that of Katsugoro, as described by Ducasse. In this case a young Japanese boy claimed to remember some details of his preceding life, which had terminated a few years earlier when he had died of smallpox at age six. "He described his burial," Ducasse writes, "the appearance of his former parents, and their house. He eventually was taken to their village, where such persons were found. He himself led the way to their house and recognized them; and they confirmed the facts he had related" (p. 24).

In sum, Ducasse allows that "continuousness of memory . . . is . . . significant for *consciousness* of one's identity" (p. 28, my italics), but he evidently holds that reincarnation makes sense even if we suppose that upon the death of one of our bodies we henceforth remember nothing of our experiences up to that point and that after the birth of our next one we remember nothing of the experiences we have had, if any, *between* these two successive incarnations. But in a later work[4] Ducasse nevertheless points out that if we wish to speak of reincarnation in a case where memories of a previous life are entirely absent we cannot properly say that what has become reincarnated is a *mind*. "It can," he observes, "be only the 'seed' left by an earlier mind—a seed consisting of the set of what . . . we have described as the set of its *basic aptitudes*; that is, of its capacities to acquire under respectively appropriate circumstances various more determinate kinds of capacities."[5]

The themes of the Foerster lecture were repeated and in some cases appreciably elaborated in Ducasse's 1949 Carus Lectures, published two years later as *Nature, Mind, and Death.*[6] In the latter, it is the final three chapters that provide a discussion of the survival problem and it is these chapters that Professor H. H. Price, reviewing the book for the *Journal of Parapsychology* in 1952, cited as its most interesting and original part. In both these works Ducasse maintains a non-committal attitude as to whether survival is a fact. Evidently he was then disinclined to say more than that it is theoretically possible. By 1958, however, in the earliest of the three papers presented here, he expresses what amounts to a belief in the *de facto* probability of survival, a conclusion that is reiterated in his most outstanding treatment of the survival problem, *A Critical Examination of the Belief in a Life After Death*, published in 1961.[4] That work includes a broad and detailed exploration of many of the themes already noted, as well as others contained in the papers that follow, and the question of reincarnation in particular is subjected to a trenchant and highly interesting analysis. Thus it is a book to which a reader may be confidently referred should he seek a fuller understanding of Ducasse's answer to the question posed in the third of our three papers: "How good is the evidence for survival after death?" That answer, as we have indicated, seems to be: "Good enough to warrant a rational belief that survival is at least slightly more probable than non-survival."

To the question posed in the second paper—"What would constitute conclusive evidence for survival after death?"—Ducasse's answer is perhaps less definite. But what mainly impresses us here is the strong reaffirmation that the question of the occurrence of survival is fundamentally empirical, and Ducasse's seeming belief that conclusive evidence[7] for or against an affirmative answer can be found through parapsychological research. In accordance with such a belief, he indicates circumstances in which we should properly feel that a conclusive case for survival after death had been made out. I think it is less clear what he would regard as conclusive evidence for *non*-survival, but we can at least infer from the paper that for Ducasse a major part of obtaining such evidence would be to conduct certain kinds of psychical research, including some of the very kinds that have already been conducted, and *not* to obtain certain kinds of results, including kinds that have already been obtained and that he has cited as being indicative of the probability of survival, *or* to obtain them but to find also that they could very plausibly be explained in terms of ESP among the living. The kinds of results in question, which Ducasse does not think can very plausibly be explained in such terms, are strongly exemplified in the seventh and longest section of the first of the three present papers: "Paranormal phenomena, science, and life after death."

This lecture, given originally at Vassar College in 1962, is such a concise, informative, and discerning an introduction to the subject that it is little wonder that Ducasse, in response to enthusiastic calls, had to repeat it at several other colleges and universities. It is here being published for the first time, however, and the Parapsychology Foundation is to be congratulated on now putting it into print.

Finally, as one surveys the many philosophical contributions to the survival problem made by Ducasse through books, lectures, essays, reviews, etc., it is natural to ask what, in the main, so much work has accomplished. The answer, as I see it, is that it has accomplished a great deal. And this may be illustrated by itemizing the principal effects of Ducasse's writings in this area. I submit, then, that they have:

(1) Gone far to expose the ambiguities and obscurities latent in the question of survival and to clarify many of the specific issues and possibilities involved.

(2) Illuminated the connections between the survival question and the several traditional accounts of the nature of mind and of the mind-body relationship given by philosophers.

(3) Facilitated the distinction between the logical and scientific aspects of the problem by discriminating the logical possibility of survival, its empirical possibility, and its reality.

(4) Confuted the view that survival is logically impossible.

(5) Accentuated the need for a parapsychological approach to the problem, and the promise of such an approach.

(6) Challenged the interested to examine afresh the scientific force of some salient putative evidence already recorded in the annals of the field.

Unfortunately, few recent philosophers have applied their craftsmanship to the problem of survival. But all of us who desire to see progress towards its solution should be well pleased that a thinker of Ducasse's power and aliveness has been among them. He has applied himself to the problem with results of enduring value. When exhibiting various forms that survival might take, he has said that in one of these forms "the occupation of the surviving person could consist in reviewing memories, reflecting upon them, extracting from them such wisdom as reflection can yield. . . ."[8] Uninviting? Perhaps. But if eventually we are so occupied, will there be time as well for a ghostly salute to Ducasse's prescience? Meanwhile, in any case, his writings on this issue, as on so many others, always themselves repay reviewing. So let us reflect on them, then, and extract the considerable wisdom they can yield. Our reflections can begin profitably with the ensuing collection.

J. M. O. WHEATLEY

Department of Philosophy
University of Toronto
Toronto 5, Canada

NOTES AND REFERENCES

1. RUSSELL, B.: *Human Knowledge: Its Scope and Limits.* London: George Allen and Unwin Ltd., 1948. The quotations in this paragraph are from p. 5.
2. For a sixteen-page list of Ducasse's publications from 1912 to the mid-sixties, as well as a short but useful biographical account, the reader may consult F. C. Dommeyer, ed., *Current Philosophical Issues: Essays in Honor of Curt John Ducasse* (Springfield, Illinois: Charles C Thomas, 1966).
3. DUCASSE, C. J.: *Is a Life after Death Possible?* Berkeley and Los Angeles: University of California Press, 1948, p. 20.
4. ———: *A Critical Examination of the Belief in a Life After Death.* Springfield, Illinois: Charles C Thomas, 1961.
5. *Ibid.,* p. 307.
6. DUCASSE, C. J.: *Nature, Mind and Death.* La Salle, Illinois: Open Court Publishing Company, 1951.
7. The term "conclusive evidence" is used by Ducasse in this context, I believe, in the sense in which we could, but might not, have conclusive evidence that at a certain site at a certain time an underground nuclear explosion took place—not in the sense some philosophers have given it when they have held that conclusive evidence is possible in the case of allegedly incorrigible *sense-datum* propositions, but not in the case of other factual propositions.
8. *Is a Life After Death Possible?* p. 21.

[15]

PARANORMAL PHENOMENA, SCIENCE, AND LIFE AFTER DEATH [1]

1. "PARANORMAL" PHENOMENA

From ancient times to the present, and from all parts of the world, reports have come of the sporadic occurrence of phenomena of various queer kinds: for instance, *apparitions* of the dead or dying; *communications* purportedly from gods, demons, or spirits of the dead; veridical *visions or dreams of events as yet future, or inaccessible in space*; the *rising* and moving unaccountably through the air of human bodies or other heavy objects; *immunity* of human bodies to *fire*; startlingly sudden *healings* of diseases or injuries; and so on.

Citation at this point of two well-attested instances of such phenomena will provide a concrete introduction to what is to follow. The first example will illustrate a phenomenon reported of many saints or mystics, namely, *levitation*—the spontaneous rising and floating of their bodies in the air.

One of the most famous of the levitating saints was St. Joseph of Copertino, a Franciscan friar who lived in the first half of the seventeenth century, and whose numerous levitations were witnessed by many persons. A book published a few years ago—*Some Human Oddities,* by E. J. Dingwall—which quotes from the documents of the time, informs us that on one occasion a priest, Antonio Chiarello, who was walking in the garden with Joseph "remarked how beautiful was the heaven which God had made. Thereupon Joseph, as if these words were an invitation to him from above, uttered a shriek, sprang from the ground and flew into the air, only coming to rest on the top of an olive tree where he remained in a kneeling position for half an hour."[2]

---

[1] Lecture first given at Vassar College, February 14, 1962.
[2] Published by Home and Van Thal, London, 1947.

The other paranormal occurrence I shall cite here is that of the often mentioned precognitive dream of Mrs. Atlay, wife of the Bishop of Hereford in England, who in 1893 wrote to F. W. H. Myers as follows:

"I dreamt that the Bishop being from home, we were unable to have family prayers as usual in the chapel, but that I read them in the large hall of the Palace, out of which, on one side, a door opens into the dining room. In my dream, prayers being ended, I left the hall, opened the dining room door, and there saw, to my horror, standing between the table and the side board, an enormous pig. The dream was very vivid and amused me much. The Bishop being from home, when dressed I went down into the hall to read prayers. The servants had not come in, so I told my governess and children, who were already there, about my dream, which amused them as much as it had done me. The servants came in and I read prayers, after which the party dispersed. I opened the dining room door, where, to my amazement, stood the pig in the very spot in which I had seen him in my dream."[3]

The governess added her own written statement that Mrs. Atlay had related the dream when she came into the hall before prayers; and inquiries by Myers disclosed that the pig escaped from its sty only while prayers were being read. Its escape was made possible by the fact that the gardener, who was then cleaning the sty, had left the gate imperfectly closed, and its entry into the Palace by the fact that the servants had left the doors open.

Of course, the veridicality of some dreams of external events as yet future is usually explicable simply as coincidence, because the events dreamed—such as the unexpected arrival of a friend—are of frequent occurrence anyway. But the presence of a large pig between the table and the side board of the dining room of an episcopal palace immediately after morning prayers is altogether in another category. It is not only a highly specific sort of event, but one so out of the ordinary as to be probably unique in the history of the earth. Coincidence is therefore not a plausible explanation.

Extraordinary occurrences such as the two just cited have often been called *supernatural*. Today, however, any of them that are not

---

[3] *Proc.* S.P.R., Vol. 11, 1895, p. 487.

illusions or fakes but really occur are assumed by scientific investigators to be just as *natural* as the many familiar phenomena whose laws we have come to understand. The paradoxical occurrences in view are therefore termed *paranormal* instead of supernatural; or, because they usually seem to manifest intelligence or purposiveness, they are also called "psychic," "metapsychic," or "parapsychological." The comprehensive, neutral term, "paranormal," means, however, simply that the phenomena so designated *transgress* the limits of what present scientific and ordinary opinion regards as *possible*.

Concerning the limits of possibility, Prof. C. D. Broad of Cambridge University has pointed out that there are certain principles which "we unhesitatingly take for granted as the framework within which all our practical activities and our scientific theories are confined." He calls them *"basic limiting principles"* because they *define the limits of what we regard as possible*. An example would be the principle that an event cannot "begin to have any effect before it has happened,"[4] and hence that an event which, as of now, has not occurred cannot possibly *cause now a perception* of it to occur to us.

Another of those "basic limiting principles" would be that one person can know another person's mental states only by perceiving bodily signs of them. This, evidently, would rule out the possibility of *telepathy*. Still another limiting principle would be that a person can perceive physical objects or events only if they stimulate his body's sense organs and thereby his brain, and hence that there can be no such thing as *clairvoyance*. And so on.

Paranormal events, then, are *events that violate* one or another of such basic limiting principles and thereby show that although the validity of those principles is *very wide,* nevertheless, contrary to what contemporary science assumes, their validity has limits: exceptions to them do occur.

Notwithstanding this, citations of paranormal phenomena continue to be ignored by most scientists. What accounts for this is that, instead of aiding to solve the problems on which scientists are at work *within* the field defined by the limiting principles, paranormal phenomena on the contrary call for expansion of the limits of that field and for attention to scientific problems that arise outside it. But,

---

[4] *The Philosophy of C. D. Broad,* ed. by P. A. Schilpp, Tudor Publishing Co., New York, 1959, p. 376.

rather than to admit that the horizon of present day science leaves out some facts and therefore needs expansion, most scientists virtuously avert their eyes when their attention is invited to those disturbing facts, and dismiss them *a priori,* or at best with perfunctory investigation.

Yet, again and again in the history of science, attention to little facts that stubbornly resisted fitting into the science of the time have, when studied, led to revolutionary advances in scientific knowledge: The road along which science has progressed is strewn with the corpses of impossibilities asserted by the scientific authorities of the respective times.

Scientific conservatism, however, is not the only source of bias where paranormal phenomena are concerned. Conservatism makes for gratuitous incredulity, but the love of the marvelous, present in many persons, on the contrary makes for equally gratuitous credulity. And particular religious beliefs or disbeliefs, which a person absorbed in childhood from his family environment, may make him later irrationally credulous, or as the case may be, irrationally incredulous, of reports of paranormal occurrences.

2. THE SOCIETIES FOR PSYCHICAL RESEARCH

The name by which the scientific investigation of paranormal phenomena has come to be known is *Psychical Research,* or more recently, *Parapsychology,* as emphasizing the experimental approach to certain of the paranormal occurrences.

Appreciation of the potentially great importance of those occurrences for science, for philosophy, and for certain aspects of religion led to the founding of the *Society for Psychical Research* in England, in 1882. The list of its presidents has since included such eminent men as the physicists Sir William Crookes, Sir Oliver Lodge, Sir William Barrett, and Lord Rayleigh; the psychologists William James, R. H. Thouless, William McDougall, and Gardner Murphy; the philosophers Henry Sidgwick, Henri Bergson, F. C. S. Schiller, C. D. Broad and H. H. Price; the classical scholars Gilbert Murray and F. W. H. Myers; the mathematician S. G. Soal; the astronomers Camille Flammarion and F. J. M. Stratton; the physiologist Charles Richet; the biologist Hans Driesch; and a number of other likewise distinguished persons.

A similar society in this country, the American Society for Psychical Research, celebrated its fiftieth anniversary a few years ago. Other such societies exist in various countries and, like the two already named, publish Journals and Proceedings. In recent times several additional organizations for research in the field of the paranormal have come into existence in the United States. One of the most active is the *Parapsychology Foundation* in New York, which has organized and subsidized several international conferences. It publishes the *International Journal of Parapsychology,* and a *Newsletter.* It also carries on research, experimental and other, in the field of the paranormal. More recently, the *Parapsychological Association* was established; and still more recently, the *Psychical Research Foundation,* dedicated specially to investigation of the question of life after death. But one of the more notable events in the history of parapsychology was the establishment in the 1930's of the *Parapsychology Laboratory* at Duke University,* headed by Prof. J. B. Rhine, whose experimental techniques have definitely established the reality of extrasensory perception and have been widely employed in other laboratories.

Work in the field of the paranormal is now carried on in a number of universities and colleges in the United States and abroad: at the University of Utrecht in Holland; at St. Joseph's College in Philadelphia; at the University of Minnesota, the University of Pittsburgh, Brown University; at the College of the City of New York, which is now offering two fellowships for work in parapsychology leading to the M.A. degree in psychology; and at still other academic institutions.

3. THE CHIEF KINDS OF PARANORMAL PHENOMENA

Before proceeding to cite additional cases of paranormal phenomena, it will be well now first to mention briefly their chief kinds.

Some paranormal phenomena are *physical,* some *mental,* and some partly each. Again, some of them occur *spontaneously,* but certain of them sometimes under *experimental* conditions. And some, which may be physical, mental, or both, are also *mediumistic,* in the

---

* Dr. J. B. Rhine established in August, 1962, a new organization, the Foundation for Research on the Nature of Man (Durham, N.C.), which houses the Institute for Parapsychology.

[21]

sense that their occurrence depends somehow on the presence of a person having special endowments.

Such a person is what the term *"medium"* now generally designates, although, it originally meant that the person concerned was assumed to the functioning as *intermediary* for communication between the living and the spirits of the dead. Some of the persons purporting to be mediums are little else than tricksters. Some, however, have certain paranormal gifts, but occasionally cheat consciously or unconsciously when those gifts, which are not under their control, happen not to be functioning. Thus, to divide persons purported to be mediums into *honest* and *dishonest* ones would be as naive as it would be so to divide men in general, or to divide men into *truth tellers* and *liars*. What is important for scientific purposes about a given medium is not whether some, perhaps many, of the phenomena which occur in his presence are spurious, but whether *any* of them, perhaps only a few, are *genuinely paranormal*.

Turning now specifically to paranormal *physical* phenomena, the chief kinds of them which have been reported are the following. Besides *levitation* already mentioned, there is also *telekinesis* or *psychokinesis*; that is, causation of motion of objects other than by any of the means or forces known to science. Telekinesis would thus include cases of so-called *poltergeist* phenomena. Other physical phenomena would be *raps, noises,* or *voices,* similarly inexplicable. Again, temporary *immunity of the body to fire,* or to *poisons; materializations* out of nothing of parts or wholes of human bodies; *apports,* for example the paradoxical coming into a wholly closed room or box of a bunch of flowers or other physical object. Again, the emanation from the body of an entranced medium of a mysterious substance, which has been called *ectoplasm,* and which takes various forms and various consistencies. Also to be mentioned are paranormally sudden *healings* of injuries, diseases, or infirmities.

The chief species of paranormal *mental* phenomena, on the other hand, are first the various forms of *extrasensory perception*: *telepathy, clairvoyance, precognition, object-reading*. Again, *apparitions* of the dead or the living; also, *out-of-the-body* experiences, in which a person finds himself observing his body from a point in space more or less distant from it, as he normally can observe the bodies of other persons. Also, temporary *possession* of a person's body by a personality other than his own; and lastly, there are the many *communications,* through an automatist or an entranced medium, purportedly made by the spirits of the dead.

4. THE QUESTIONS RELEVANT TO REPORTS OR PERCEPTIONS OF OSTENSIBLY PARANORMAL OCCURRENCES

Evidently, to persons whose interest in paranormal phenomena is the scientific interest, the crucial question concerning reports or observations of them is whether they were *really paranormal* in the sense defined by Professor Broad, or only seemed to be so. The answer in any given case depends on such considerations as the following:

Was the *reporter* of the phenomenon *truthful?* If so, is his report *objective,* i.e., limited to what he *actually observed,* as distinguished from what he may have taken it to signify? Is the report *precise, detailed,* and *comprehensive;* or vague, superficial, and partial? Is the report *a record made at the time?* or if not, then *how soon after?* Or is it *based only on present memory?*

Again, was the *observer* of the phenomenon *competent;* i.e., did he possess the perhaps *special critical equipment* needed for dependable observation under the circumstances that existed? For example, familiarity with *conjuring tricks and accessories;* and familiarity with the *psychology of illusions of perception?*

And if the phenomenon reported or observed was genuinely paranormal, the question remains as to *what then it signifies.* For example, does an apparition of a deceased person, or a message received through a medium allegedly from such a person, signify that *survival after death* is a fact? Or is some other interpretation of it possible?

5. SOME NOTABLE INSTANCES OF PARANORMAL PHYSICAL PHENOMENA

Having now called attention to the various cautions to which acceptance of reports of paranormal phenomena is properly subject, I next proceed to cite certain of the concrete cases that are both most impressive and hardest to reject in view of the evidence for them.

First some cases of *levitation.* When, at the beginning of my remarks, I cited the levitations of St. Joseph of Copertino, the fact

[23]

naturally came to mind that, under the influence of religious emotion and of devotion to religious beliefs, human beings easily become unreliable observers, easy prey to suggestion, or even prone to stretch the truth if need be for the greater glory of God; and that this may well account for the reports of the saint's levitations.

Nevertheless there is, for the fact that levitation sometimes occurs, testimony which cannot be dismissed on the grounds of religious bias, or of love of the marvelous, or of suggestibility, or of inadequate opportunity to observe; testimony, indeed, which is about as strong as human testimony ever gets. In the case I shall now cite, the body levitated was that of the famous medium, D. D. Home. The person who witnessed the levitations and reports them was the eminent physicist and chemist, Sir William Crookes. The place where they occurred was the dining room of Crookes' own house, where only personal friends of his were present besides the medium. And they occurred in good light. Crookes writes:

"The best cases of Home's levitations I witnessed were in my own house. On one occasion he went to a clear part of the room, and after standing quietly for a minute, told us he was rising. I saw him slowly rise up with a continuous gliding movement and remain about six inches off the ground for several seconds, when he slowly descended. On this occasion no one moved from their places. On another occasion I was invited to come to him, when he rose 18 inches off the ground, and I passed my hand under his feet, round him, and over his head when he was in the air.

"On several occasions Home and the chair on which he was sitting at the table rose off the ground. This was generally done very deliberately, and Home sometimes then tucked up his feet on the seat of the chair and held up his hands in view of all of us. On such an occasion I have got down and seen and felt that all four legs were off the ground at the same time, Home's feet being on the chair. Less frequently the levitating power extended to those sitting next to him. Once my wife was thus raised off the ground in her chair."[5]

Again Crookes writes:

"One of the most striking things I ever saw in the way of movements of light objects was when a glass water-bottle and tumbler

---

[5] *Jour.* S.P.R., Vol. 6, 1893-1894, pp. 341-342.

rose from the table. There was plenty of light in the room from two large salted alcohol flames, and Home's hands were not near. The bottle and glass floated about over the middle of the table. I asked whether they would answer questions by knocking one against the other. Immediately three taps together signified 'Yes.' They then kept floating about six or eight inches up, going from the front of one sitter to another round the table, tapping together and answering questions in this manner. Quite five minutes were occupied by this phenomenon, during which time we had ample opportunity of seeing that Home was a passive agent, and that no wires or strings, &c., were in use. But the idea of any such tricks was absurd, as the occurrence was in my own house, and no one could have tampered with anything in the room, Home not having been in the room till we all came in together for the séance."[6]

Crookes adds that, "In almost all the séances he had with Home there was plenty of light to see all that occurred, and not only to enable me to write down notes of what was taking place but to read my notes without difficulty."[7]

Concerning Home's levitations, Crookes writes elsewhere: "There are at least a hundred recorded instances of Mr. Home's rising off the ground, in the presence of as many separate persons. . . . To reject the recorded evidence on this subject is to reject all human testimony whatever; for no fact in sacred or profane history is supported by a stronger array of proofs."[8]

Another extraordinary physical phenomenon is the *temporary immunity* of the body to *fire*. Concerning this, Crookes writes:

"Mr. Home again went to the fire, and after stirring the hot coals about with his hand, took out a red-hot piece nearly as big as an orange, and putting it on his right hand, covered it over with his left hand so as to almost completely enclose it, and then blew into the small furnace thus extemporised until the lump of charcoal was nearly white-hot, and then drew my attention to the lambent flame . . . licking round his fingers."[9]

[6] *Ibid.*, pp. 342-343.

[7] *Ibid.*, p. 344.

[8] *Quarterly Jour. of Science*, January, 1874.

[9] *Proc.* S.P.R., Vol. 6, 1889-1890, p. 103.

Another witness, Lord Adare, relates another similar occurrence at the house of a friend of his. He writes: "Home then went into a trance. He walked about the room . . . he went back to the fire, and with his hand stirred the embers into a flame; then kneeling down, he placed his face right among the burning coals, moving it about as though bathing it in water. Then, getting up, he held his finger for some time in the flame of the candle."[10]

Home was able to confer temporarily on others the same immunity to fire. Lord Lindsay writes as follows concerning his own experience of this: "Eight times, I myself have held a red-hot coal in my hands without injury, when it scorched my face on raising my hand. Once, I wished to see if they really would burn, and I said so, and touched a coal with the middle finger of my right hand, and I got a blister as large as a sixpence; I instantly asked him [Home] to give me the coal, and I held the part that burnt me, in the middle of my hand, for three or four minutes, without the least inconvenience."[11]

To these cases dating back to the end of the nineteenth century, I may add those which occur today among the members of a certain religious sect located in the mountains of Kentucky. Some of them were witnessed by a New Jersey psychiatrist, Dr. Berthold E. Schwartz, who reports them and presents photographs of them in an article entitled "Ordeal by Serpents, Fire, and Strychnine," published in the July 1960 issue of the *Psychiatric Quarterly*. The photographs show a thumb and a foot being held in the flame of a coal oil torch. Some members of the sect, while in trance, were also seen by Dr. Schwartz to handle rattlesnakes and copperheads without harm; and also to swallow without ill effects doses of strychnine sulphate that would ordinarily be lethal.

Many other cases of well-attested paranormal physical phenomena could be cited, but I shall mention only one more. It was related to me by the late Hereward Carrington, who had participated in it himself. It occurred in Naples in 1907, when he and two other members of a research committee of the Society for Psychical Research were investigating the Italian medium, Eusapia Palladino.

---

[10] *Proc.* S.P.R., Vol. 35, 1926, pp. 133-135.
[11] *Report of the London Dialectical Society's Committee on Spiritualism,* Longmans, Green, Reader and Dyer, London, 1871, p. 208.

233306

Carrington told me that on one occasion Eusapia had been holding her hand some distance above a stool which stood on the floor, and that, as she moved her hand about, the stool on the floor followed the motions of the hand. Then she turned to Carrington and said: "Now *you* do it"; and put her hand on his shoulder. He then moved his hand about, above the stool, which followed its motions as it had done those of Eusapia's hand.

6. INSTANCES OF PARANORMAL MENTAL PHENOMENA

I turn next to some instances of paranormal *mental* phenomena. Those which have attracted the most attention during the last 25 years have been extrasensory perceptions—especially clairvoyance, telepathy, and precognition—as demonstrated by statistical evaluation of the results of long series of careful experiments with Zener cards; these come in packs of 25 and bear one or another of five symbols: a star, circle, cross, square, and wavy lines. This card-guessing technique was devised by Prof. J. B. Rhine at Duke University and has been widely adopted since then. It is not spectacular and does not lend itself to brief or non-technical description on such an occasion as the present; but the contribution it has made to scientific proof that extrasensory perception really occurs has been epoch-making.

I shall mention only the experience with it of the mathematician, S. G. Soal, of the University of London, who had made many hundreds of card-guessing experiments in the attempt to duplicate in England the results obtained by Rhine and Pratt at Duke University, but who had consistently failed to get results that chance could not account for. One day, however, another experimenter, Whately Carington, urged Soal to go back over his records and see whether the guesses that had been made had not perhaps been guesses *not* of the card that was the *actual* target, but of the card—at that time unknown to anybody—that was next going to be the target, or perhaps that had been the target for the preceding guess.

When Soal reexamined his records with this possibility in mind, he found that, in the case of two of his subjects, Mrs. Stewart and Basil Shackleton, the numbers of guesses correct for the preceding card, or for the card that would next be the target, exceeded by millions to one what chance could have accounted for. What the experiments had actually demonstrated thus turned out to have been

[27]

not clairvoyance of the target, but retrocognition or precognition.[12]

As an instance of *spontaneous* as distinguished from experimental extrasensory perception, I shall mention only a case which came under my own notice. It is that of the wife of a friend of mine, Prof. F. C. Dommeyer, head of the Philosophy Department at San Jose State College. For more than 20 years his wife's dreams had occasionally contained a certain feature; and whenever this occurred, she then received invariably within a week, but usually in a few hours or a day or two, some money that she had had no reason to expect. When Dommeyer mentioned this to me, I suggested that, next time his wife told him she had just had such a dream, he should write the fact on a postcard addressed to the American Society for Psychical Research and immediately mail it at the post office, so that the postmark would be evidence that the dream had occurred *before*, rather than perhaps only after the coming of the money. Shortly after this, I took a dollar bill, put it in an envelope which I sealed and sent to a friend in another city, asking him to address it to Mrs. Dommeyer and mail it; and saying that I would tell him later why I asked him to do this. In a few days, the A.S.P.R. received a postcard from Prof. Dommeyer stating that his wife had just had a dream containing the predictive feature. The envelope containing the dollar bill reached Mrs. Dommeyer about three hours after the postcard recording her dream had been mailed. This case, and four other cases of her dream, are reported by Prof. Dommeyer in an article which appeared in the July 1955 issue of the *Journal* of the A.S.P.R.

7. INSTANCES OF PARANORMAL OCCURRENCES SUGGESTIVE OF SURVIVAL AFTER DEATH

Among paranormal mental phenomena, however, some of the most impressive to the persons who experience them are those which they have assumed to constitute evidence of survival of the human personality after death. Notable among these are the *apparitions of the dead,* commonly referred to as "ghosts."

An especially well evidenced case is that of the "Morton Ghost." Miss Morton was at that time a medical student and viewed the

---

[12] *Modern Experiments in Telepathy,* by S. G. Soal and F. Bateman, Yale University Press, New Haven, 1954, pp. 123-128.

apparitions without fear or nervousness but only with scientific curiosity.

She states that, having one evening gone up to her room, she heard someone at the door, opened it, and saw in the passage the figure of a tall lady, dressed in black, whose face was hidden by a handkerchief held in her right hand. She descended the stairs and Miss Morton followed; but the small piece of candle she carried went out, and she returned to her room. The figure was seen again half a dozen times during the next two years by Miss Morton, once by her sister Mrs. K., once by the housemaid, and once by Miss Morton's brother and by a boy. After the first apparition Miss Morton made it a practice to follow the figure downstairs into the drawing room. She spoke to the apparition but never got any reply; she cornered it several times in order to touch it, but it then simply disappeared. Its footsteps were audible and characteristic, and were heard by Miss Morton's three sisters and by the cook. Miss Morton stretched some threads across the stairs, but the figure passed right through them without detaching them. The figure was seen in the orchard by a neighbor as well as in the house by Miss Morton's sisters, by the cook, by the charwoman, by a parlormaid, and by the gardener. But Miss Morton's father could not see it, even when he was shown where it stood. The apparition was seen during the day as well as at night. In all about twenty people saw it, some of them many times; and some of them not having previously heard of the apparition or of the sounds. The figure was described in the same way by all. The apparitions continued for 7 years. The figure wore widow's cuffs and corresponded to the description of a former tenant of the house, Mrs. S., whose life there had been unhappy.[13]

Another outstanding case is that of the numerous apparitions at the beginning of the nineteenth century of the form of the deceased Mrs. Butler in a Maine village, to which the Rev. Abraham Cummings, holder of a Master of Arts degree from Brown University, had proceeded in order to expose what he had assumed must be a hoax. He writes as follows: "Some time in July 1806, in the evening I was informed by two persons that they had just seen the Spectre in the field. About ten minutes after, I went out, not to see a

13 *Proc.* S.P.R., Vol. 8, 1892, pp. 311-332.

miracle for I believed they had been mistaken. Looking toward an eminence twelve rods distance from the house, I saw there as I supposed, one of the white rocks. This confirmed my opinion of their spectre, and I paid no more attention to it. Three minutes after, I accidentally looked in the same direction, and the white rock was in the air; its form a complete globe, with a tincture of red . . . and its diameter about two feet. Fully satisfied that this was nothing ordinary I went toward it for more accurate examination. While my eye was constantly upon it, I went on four or five steps, when it came to me from the distance of eleven rods, as quick as lightning, and instantly assumed a personal form with a female dress, but did not appear taller than a girl seven years old. While I looked upon her, I said in my mind 'you are not tall enough for the woman who has so frequently appeared among us!' Immediately she grew up as large and as tall as I considered that woman to be. Now she appeared glorious. On her head was the representation of the sun diffusing the luminous, rectilinear rays every way to the ground. Through the rays I saw the personal form and the woman's dress."

In the pamphlet which the Rev. Mr. Cummings published concerning the apparitions of Mrs. Butler, he reproduces some thirty affidavits which he had obtained at the time from persons who had seen and/or heard the spectre; for the apparition spoke and delivered discourses sometimes over an hour long. She appeared "sometimes to one alone . . . sometimes to two or three; then to five or six, then to ten or twelve; again to twenty; and once to more than forty witnesses. She appeared . . . several times in the open field. There, white as the light, she moved like a cloud above the ground in personal form and magnitude, and in the presence of more than forty people. She tarried with them till after daylight, and then vanished." Several of the witnesses reported that the apparition begins as a formless small luminous cloud, which then grows and in a moment takes the form of the deceased Mrs. Butler.[14] (This incidentally was what occurred when, over fifty years ago in New York, I witnessed in red light but not under test conditions a purported materialization of a man's body.)

---

[14] *Immortality Proved by the Testimony of Sense,* by Abraham Cummings, Bath, Maine, 1826.

The *prima facie* evidence of survival provided by an apparition is most impressive when the apparition supplies information the percipient did not possess, but which he later finds to be veridical. One famous such case is that of a traveling salesman whose sister had died in 1867, and who nine years later was in his hotel room at noon in St. Joseph, Missouri, smoking a cigar and writing up the orders he had obtained. His statement reads: "I suddenly became conscious that some one was sitting on my left, with one arm resting on the table. Quick as a flash I turned and distinctly saw the form of my dead sister, and for a brief second or so looked her squarely in the face; and so sure was I that it was she, that I sprang forward in delight, calling her by name, and, as I did so, the apparition instantly vanished. . . . I was near enough to touch her . . . and noted her features, expression, and details of dress, &c. She appeared as if alive."

He was so moved by the experience that he cut his trip short and returned to his home in St. Louis, where he related the occurrence to his parents, mentioning among other details of the apparition that on the right side of the girl's nose he had noticed a bright red scratch about three-fourths of an inch long. "When I mentioned this," he states, "my mother rose trembling to her feet and nearly fainted away, and . . . exclaimed that I had indeed seen my sister, as no living mortal but herself was aware of that scratch, which she had accidentally made while doing some little act of kindness after my sister's death. She said she well remembered how pained she was to think she should have, unintentionally, marred the features of her dead daughter, and that unknown to all, how she had carefully obliterated all traces of the slight scratch with the aid of powder, &c., and that she had never mentioned it to a human being, from that day to this."[15]

Another case, interesting for a similar reason, is that of the will of James L. Chaffin, a North Carolina farmer, who in November 1905 made a will attested by two witnesses in which he left his farm to his son Marshall, the third of his four sons, and nothing to the other three sons or to his wife. In January 1919, however, he made a new will, not witnessed but legally valid because it was wholly in his

15 *Proc.* S.P.R., Vol. 6, 1889-1890, pp. 17-20.

own handwriting. In it he first stated that it was being made after his reading of the 27th chapter of Genesis; and then that he wanted his property divided equally between his four children, and that they must take care of their mother. He then placed this will at the 27th chapter of Genesis in a Bible that had belonged to his father, folding over the pages to enclose the will.

He died in 1921 without ever having mentioned to anybody the existence of the second will. The first will was not contested and was probated by its beneficiary. But some four years later the second son, James Pinkney Chaffin, began to have very vivid dreams that his father appeared to him at his bedside, without speaking. Later in June of 1925, however, the father again appeared at the bedside, wearing a familiar black overcoat, and then spoke, saying, "You will find my will in my overcoat pocket." The coat was eventually found in his brother's house, and examined. The inside lining of the inside pocket had been stitched together. On cutting the stitches, James found a little roll of paper on which, in his father's handwriting, were written only the words: "Read the 27th chapter of Genesis in my daddie's old Bible." James then returned to his mother's house, accompanied by his daughter, by a neighbor, and by the neighbor's daughter. When they found the Bible and opened it at the 27th chapter of Genesis, they found the second will. It was admitted to probate in December of the same year.[16]

Whether apparitions of the dead really are evidence for survival, however, is made dubious by the fact that there are a good many cases on record of apparitions of persons who were living and in good health at the time. Another fact, which also has to be taken into account in connection with apparitions is that they always wear clothes of some sort; and hence that, as someone has put it, if ghosts have clothes, then clothes have ghosts! This suggests that apparitions, especially when perceived by several persons, may be mental images which, strangely, have become somehow concrete enough to be visible.

Another kind of *prima facie* evidence of survival after death consists of the many communications, received by various persons over the years through mediums such as Mrs. Piper in Boston or Mrs. Leonard in London, purportedly emanating from deceased

---

[16] *Proc.* S.P.R., Vol. 36, 1926-1928, pp. 517-524.

relatives who identify themselves by mention of various details or incidents of family life sometimes not known to any living person other than the one to whom the communication is made, or else perhaps only to the person from whom he later ascertains the correctness of the details communicated. Here again, however, the evidence of such communications is weakened by the possibility that the medium, while in trance, gets the facts by telepathy from the mind of some living person who knows them, or by clairvoyance from existing records of them. Also, communications have been received through mediums from persons that purported to have died, but who in fact were alive and well at the time. Also, from various characters out of novels!

The communications most difficult to explain on any hypothesis other than that of survival, however, are those which came to be referred to as "cross correspondences." In brief and roughly, they consisted of pairs of communications by automatic writing, each through a different automatist; and each of the communications being unintelligible by itself. But the two, when put together, turned out to refer to some recondite passage in the Greek or Latin classics. There were many such pairs of communications during a period of several years, without possibility of collusion between the several automatists concerned.

The deceased persons from whom those quasi-jigsaw-puzzle messages purported to come were chiefly F. W. H. Myers, Edmund Gurney, Henry Sidgwick, and some others of the deceased early members of the S.P.R., who claimed to have devised this particular scheme in order to show that not only their memories survived, but also their active and purposive intelligence.

The only additional case hard to account for other than on the hypothesis of survival that I shall cite is a case of apparent *possession* of the body of a living girl for some weeks by a personality radically different from her own.

Most cases of this kind are adequately accounted for as control of the body by a temporarily dissociated part of the ordinary personality. But the case I have in view does not lend itself to this explanation inasmuch as the invading personality was definitely identified as that of a girl who had died at the age of 18, at a time when the girl whose body she invaded some twelve years later was only a year and a half old. The affair occurred in Watseka, Illinois, and the facts, which were carefully recorded and verified, were essentially as follows:

One of the girls, Mary Roff, had died at the age of 18. At that time the other, Lurancy Vennum, was only a little over one year old. When Lurancy reached the age of 14, her body, to all appearances was suddenly taken possession of by the personality of Mary Roff, who did not recognize Mr. and Mrs. Vennum or their other children or neighbors, but begged to be taken home to her parents, Mr. and Mrs. Roff, who lived some distance away and were but slightly acquainted with the Vennums. She was allowed to go and live with them, and there she knew every person and everything that Mary knew when in her original body twelve to twenty-five years before, recognizing and calling by name those who were friends and neighbors of the family at that time, and calling attention to scores of incidents that had occurred during her natural life. After some 14 weeks, however, the Mary Roff personality disappeared, and that of Lurancy Vennum returned to her own body. (The case was reported by Dr. E. W. Stevens, who had been called in when Lurancy began to act strangely, in a pamphlet entitled "The Watseka Wonder"; and is described by F. W. H. Myers in his famous work, *Human Personality and its Survival of Bodily Death*.[17]

8. CONCLUDING REMARKS

The various paranormal phenomena of which we have now considered reports are indeed hard to believe. But why? Ultimately, because they are very rare and we do not happen to have observed any of them ourselves. As Charles Richet pointed out in his presidential address to the S.P.R., belief is essentially a matter of habit: most men really believe only what they are accustomed to. Levitation, for example, is not a priori any more or any less paradoxical than gravitation. But the latter is experienced every day by each of us; whereas very few men have experienced or witnessed levitation. Hence they disbelieve that it occurs. On the other hand, however, the love of the mysterious and marvelous is strong in many persons,

---

[17] *Human Personality and its Survival of Bodily Death,* by F. W. H. Myers, Longmans, Green, and Co., New York, 1903, Vol. 1, pp. 360-368.

and, in them, it begets wishful belief of reports of paranormal oc-currences.

From attention to both of these psychological facts, an important lesson is to be learned. It is that although the evidence offered by addicts of the marvelous for the reality of the phenomena they accept must be critically examined, it is equally necessary on the other side to scrutinize just as closely and critically the skeptics' allegations of fraud, or of malobservation, or of misinterpretation of what was observed, or of hypnotically induced hallucinations. For there is likely to be just as much wishful thinking, prejudice, emotion, snap judg-ment, naïveté, and intellectual dishonesty on the side of orthodoxy, of skepticism, and of conservatism, as on the side of hunger for and belief in the marvelous. The emotional motivation for irrespon-sible disbelief is, in fact, probably even stronger—especially in scien-tifically educated persons, whose pride of knowledge is at stake—than is in other persons the motivation for irresponsible belief. In these matters, nothing is so rare as genuine objectivity and impar-tiality of judgment—judgment determined neither by the will to believe nor by the will to disbelieve, but only by the will to get at the truth irrespective of whether it turns out to be comfortably familiar or uncomfortably novel, consoling or distressing, orthodox, or un-orthodox.

In the light of all this, I can do no better than to bring these remarks to a close by two quotations. One is from Sir William Crookes who in 1889 wrote:

"Most assuredly, so far as my knowledge of science goes, there is absolutely no reason *a priori* to deny the possibility of such phe-nomena as I have described. Those who assume . . . that we are now acquainted with all, or nearly all, or even with any assignable proportion, of the forces at work in the universe, show a limitation of conception which ought to be impossible in an age when the widening of the circle of our definite knowledge does but reveal the proportionately widening circle of our blank, absolute, indubi-table ignorance."[18]

These words, let it be noted, were written at a time when the transmutation of elements was still thought to be only a dream of

---

[18] *Proc.* S.P.R., Vol. 6, 1889-1890, p. 100.

mediaeval alchemists; and radio, radar, or television did not yet exist.

The other quotation, which is to the same general effect, is from Prof. C. A. Mace, past president of the Psychology Section of the British Association.

"It is a paradox . . ." he writes, "that the defences we erect within ourselves against prejudice and superstition themselves tend so to encrust and petrify the mind that it becomes increasingly resistant to novel truths. No one has had better reason to be conscious of this paradox than the student of psychical research in his efforts to invoke co-operation from orthodox, working scientists in relevant and allied fields of investigation.[19]

---

[19] *Proc.* S.P.R., Vol. 44, 1936-1937, p. 279.

WHAT WOULD CONSTITUTE CONCLUSIVE EVIDENCE OF SURVIVAL AFTER DEATH?[1]

In the course of a lecture delivered by the writer a few years ago at a meeting of the American Society for Psychical Research, the members of the audience were invited to join in the following experiment. Let us suppose, they were told, that a friend of ours, John Doe, had been aboard an airplane which has crashed in the ocean, and that no survivors have been found; but that, some time later, our telephone rings and (a) that a voice we recognize as John Doe's is heard and a conversation with it held which convinces us that the speaker is really John Doe. Or alternatively, let us suppose (b) that the voice heard is not John Doe's but that of some other person seemingly relaying his words to us and ours to him; and that the conversation so held does convince us that the person with whom we are conversing through that intermediary is John Doe.

The question the audience was then asked to consider was, of what kind in either case must the content of that conversation have been, that made us regard as certain or highly probable that our interlocutor really was John Doe?

Obviously, the two imagined situations (a) and (b) are, in all essentials, analogues of cases where a person is conversing with the purported surviving spirit of a deceased friend who either, in case (a) "possesses" for the time being parts at least of the body of a medium, i.e., uses her auditory and her vocal organs or writing hand; or else who, in case (b), employs the medium only as intermediary, i.e., "speaks" to her telepathically and "listens," also telepathically, to what she hears when we speak.

Thus, because the John Doe case and the case of conversation

[1] Reprinted from *Journal* S.P.R., Vol. 41, No. 714, December 1962.

through a medium are complete analogues, the particular kind of content of the conversation that would be adequate to prove or make positively probable that John Doe has survived the crash would likewise be adequate to prove or make positively probable that the mind of our deceased friend has survived the death of his body.[2]

Some criticisms of this contention, however, were made in the course of informal discussions of it with interested persons; and the remarks which follow are offered as replies to those criticisms.

The first criticism was that the telephone is known to be an instrument of communication, whereas a medium is not known to be so. The reply is, of course, that such evidence of survival as the conversation may have provided consisted only of the content and style of the responses made to our own utterances, and not at all of whether those responses were emitted by a medium's organs of expression or by a telephone.

The chief other criticism was based on a statement which J. B. Rhine had made in 1956 after referring to the fact that the reality of extrasensory perception had been experimentally demonstrated— the statement, namely, that "if a medium had sufficient psi capacity, it was within the realm of possibility she could do anything through her own powers that had been considered proper to credit to the spirit communicators supposedly working through her."[3]

It was urged in the discussions that possession of such powers by the medium is a more economical explanation of the contents and style of the communications; for the medium is anyway known to exist and so is extrasensory perception; whereas the spirit survival explanation requires one to assume gratuitously (1) that spirits exist; (2) that they are capable of remembering; (3) that they are capable of temporarily "possessing" the body of some living persons; and (4) that they are capable of telepathic communication with some living persons.

Also, for the purpose of showing the spirit survival hypothesis to

---

[2] The lecture in which the John Doe analogy was set forth has been published in the *Journal* of the A.S.P.R., July 1959, under the title "How good is the evidence for survival after death?"; and the analogy has since been incorporated as Sec. 5 in Ch. XIX of the writer's *The Belief in a Life after Death*, 1961.

[3] "Research on Spirit Survival Re-examined," *Journal of Parapsychology*, June 1959, pp. 123-124.

be superfluous, cases were cited in the discussion where the communications were from wholly fictitious spirits (e.g., the John Ferguson and the Bessie Beals cases); and others where (as in the Gordon Davis case) the person purportedly deceased and communicating was in fact still living and was engaged at the time in his ordinary occupations.

The first comment these criticisms invite is that, in discussions of the question of survival, clarity of thought is promoted if, for one thing, one leaves out altogether the weasel word, "spirits," and uses instead the word "minds"; the question then being whether there is any evidence that minds that were incarnate (or some constituents of them) continue to exist and to function discarnate, thus surviving their body's death.

When the question of survival is formulated thus in terms not of "spirits" but of *minds,* then the allegation that the survival explanation makes gratuitously the four assumptions mentioned above is seen to be erroneous. For (1) that there are minds is not an assumption but a known fact; (2) that minds are capable of remembering is likewise not an assumption but is known; (3) that minds are capable of "possessing" living human bodies is also a known fact, for "possession" is but the name of the normal *relation* of a mind to its living body. *Paranormal* "possession" would be possession in the very same sense, but only temporary, and of a living body by a mind other than its own—that other mind either being one which had been that of a body now dead; or being a mind temporarily wandering from its own living body. And (4) that telepathic communication between minds is possible is also a know fact.

Once all this is clear, the only questions remaining are:

(*a*) whether it is *known to be impossible* that a mind, or some constituents of it, should continue to exist and to exercise after its body's death any of the capacities it is known to have had; and if, as actually is the case, this is *not* known to be impossible, then

(*b*) just how, otherwise than as a case of paranormal "possession" by a particular definitely identified mind having survived discarnate, is the case of for example the "Watseka Wonder" to be explained?—specifically, "possession" for some 14 weeks of the living body of Lurancy Vennum aged 14 by a mind having the complex of capacities *distinctive of the mind of Mary Roff,* whose body had

[39]

died some 12 years before at 18 years of age at a time when Lurancy was a little over 1 year old.

(c) Or, in a case not of "possession," but of conversation through an entranced medium with a mind having, as in the "Lethe" case, certain scholarly capacities that together were distinctive of the mind of F. W. H. Myers, but were not possessed by the mind of Mrs. Piper who was the medium; how is this to be explained otherwise than on the hypothesis that the conversation was with Myers' mind surviving discarnate?

In such cases, the paranormal "possession," or the utterance paranormally by the medium of opposite scholarly or expert technical contributions to a conversation, which contributions her mind is known not to have been equipped to make, does not *postulate* or *assume* that the particular identified mind concerned survives, but *evidences,* more or less positively, that that particular mind survives.

It evidences it unless certain paranormal capacities known to exist in some persons would, if present in the "possessed" person's own mind, or in the medium's own mind, provide an alternative explanation. The paranormal capacities needed for this, however, could not consist merely of extrasensory perception, since *perception,* whether sensory or extrasensory, is only of *particular* physical events or objects, or of *particular* mental events or states. Nor, for the same reason, could the needed capacities consist merely of even super ESP—"super" in the sense of extending to particular events, objects, or states more numerous, or more hidden, or more distant in time or space, than ESP is yet known to be capable of detecting.

For, in addition and crucially, the paranormal capacities needed for alternative explanation of cases such as that of the "Watseka Wonder" or the "Lethe" case must include presence in the "possessed" person's or the medium's own mind of capacities that are *not common* like the capacity to remember, but that are *idiosyncratic* whether jointly or singly; and therefore insofar identify the particular mind that has them, much as fingerprints identify the particular human body that made them on a glass or mirror—it being pretty definitely known, moreover, that the medium, or the person whose body is seemingly "possessed" by the particular mind known to have had those highly special capacities, never had the opportunity of acquiring them. And further, the fact being that there exists no experimental evidence of its being possible to acquire duplicates of these highly identificatory capacities paranormally; nor any anecdotal evidence of such possibility, other than that which the various anecdotes which are the very ones to be explained would provide if, but only if, they had themselves *already* been authoritatively explained.

Thus, when Occam's razor is alleged to shave off survival as a superfluous hypothesis, and to leave ESP as sufficient to account for all the facts in evidence, it turns out that ESP cannot do it without being arbitrarily endowed with an *ad hoc* "beard" consisting not of capacity for more far-reaching *perception,* but of capacity for reasoning, inventing, constructing, understanding, judging; i.e., for *active thinking*; and more specifically for the particular modes of such active thinking which *only* the particular mind whose survival is in question is *known* to have been equipped with.

As regards the unconscious creating by a medium's mind of fictitious personalities (e.g., the John Ferguson personality), or the unconscious impersonation by the medium of personalities that exist or have existed and which the medium has clairvoyantly or telepathically observed or learned something about (as, e.g., in the Gordon Davis case), no difficulty is involved any more than in the case of what a writer of fiction invents; or of what an actor does who, in a play, impersonates some historical character. For it is easy for the inventor of fiction to make his hero say, and to remember having made him say, things which the novelist was himself equipped to say; and easy likewise for the actor to imitate gestures, intonations, pet phrases, and other *perceptible* behaviors, which he had himself observed or learned of as peculiar to the historical character concerned. Cases such as those two are not the ones for explanation of which the survival hypothesis appears to be needed.

But note how radically different would be the task of a novelist or of an actor having himself no knowledge of, let us say, theoretical physics, if he were to try to invent, or to improvise an impersonation of, such a contribution to a conversation on theoretical physics as Einstein would be equipped to make. Or, to take a case on record instead of this imaginary one, consider the "Lethe" case and the answers made by the purported surviving Myers, through the pencil and the vocal organs of Mrs. Piper, to the questions asked by G. B.

Dorr. Is it in the least plausible that Mrs. Piper—a woman of limited education—not only herself had or got by ESP the knowledge of the recondite details of Ovid's writings required for the allusions made by the purported Myers—some of which knowledge Dorr did not himself have; but in addition herself had and exercised the capacity which Myers had (but which event Mrs. Verrall, who was a lecturer in classics at Newnham College, said she herself did not have) so to combine those allusions as to make them say together tacitly about Lethe something which Myers knew, but which was other than any of the things which, singly, those allusions referred to; and which it took Piddington much study and thought to identify?

To account for such an ingenious feat of inventive and constructive activity as the purported Myers performed in this case, something different from ESP *in kind,* not just in degree, is indispensable; namely, either Myers' own mind at work, or else a duplicate of it; which, however, then needs to be itself accounted for.

Of course, that something different in kind from ESP is needed to account for the cross-correspondences has been pointed out before —for instance by Kenneth Richmond (*Evidence of Identity,* p. 76), and by H. F. Saltmarsh (*Evidence of Personal Survival,* pp. 32 ff.) who, moreover, in order to bring home to his readers how difficult a task is the constructing of a cross-correspondence, invites them to try it and gives them instructions as to how to proceed (p. 149).

The contribution additional to these, which the present paper attempts to make to the discussion of the survival explanation of some of the cases on record, consists in formulation—so clear as to prevent henceforth certain fatal confusions—of a distinction which is crucial, and which has been felt and tacitly depended on whenever the evidence of a person's identity has been held to consist ultimately of such special knowledge as that person is known to have possessed.

That all-important distinction is the distinction between knowledge in the sense of knowledge *that . . . ,* and knowledge in the sense of knowledge *how to. . . .*

In the first of these two senses, the knowledge possessed consists of *items of information;* and these might conceivably get perceived in their possessor by a medium, extrasensorily.

In the second of the two senses, on the other hand, the knowledge possessed consists of *mental skills;* and although a medium not herself possessing a particular mental skill may be able to *infer,* from sensory or extrasensory perception of manifestations of exercise of it by another person, that that other person possesses it, nevertheless the perceiving of those manifestations does not endow the medium herself with the particular mental skill concerned.

The most which perception of those manifestations of it can enable the medium to do is to enact approximate imitations of some of those manifestations—which imitations, however, are likely to be inapposite to their particular context in the conversation taking place at the time. Examples of just this would be provided by, among others, instances of xenoglossy merely *recitative,* as distinguished from intelligently *responsive.*

HOW GOOD IS THE EVIDENCE FOR SURVIVAL AFTER DEATH?[1]

Many attempts have been made by philosophers and theologians to prove that the soul of man is immortal, but the premises from which their arguments deduce this conclusion turn out when scrutinized to be altogether "iffy." They are wishful beliefs rather than propositions known to be true, and the ingenious arguments based on them therefore really establish nothing.

On the other hand, it has been contended that modern biology and psychology have shown that consciousness is wholly a product of the activity of the body and more particularly of the brain, and hence cannot possibly continue after the body has died.

But the question how body and mind are related cannot be responsibly answered without thoroughgoing preliminary analysis of the concepts of "body," "mind," "life," and "causality," and the need for this analysis is commonly ignored by those who, merely on the basis of experiments on the body, assert that survival of consciousness after death is impossible. That analysis unfortunately is too lengthy and technical to permit of introducing it here. Hence I can say only that, in the light of it, and after careful scrutiny of all the evidence which allegedly proves that survival is impossible, the evidence falls in my judgment far short of establishing the impossibility. Rather, the conclusion that survival is impossible is but a gratuitously materialistic wide extrapolation of the conclusion which the evidence would really warrant.[2]

---

[1] Paper presented by Professor Ducasse at a meeting of the Society for Psychical Research on November 12, 1958. Reprinted from *Journal* A.S.P.R., Vol. 53, July, 1959, pp. 90-105.

[2] The various considerations alleged to rule out the possibility of survival may be found—presented readably but with materialist fervor rather than logical rigor—in Corliss Lamont's *The Illusion of Immortality* (Philosophical Library, New York, 1950).

On the present occasion, then, it will be taken as a fact that survival of consciousness after death has not been shown either to be necessarily true or to be impossible. This means that, so far as anybody has yet shown to the contrary, such survival remains possible: possible *theoretically* because the supposition of it is not internally contradictory; and possible *empirically* in that the supposition is not incompatible with anything definitely known.

1. SURVIVAL AN EMPIRICAL BUT AMBIGUOUS QUESTION

The question whether survival is a fact is therefore one which, if it can be responsibly answered at all, has to be answered on the basis of whatever empirical evidence of survival may be available. But the *meaning* of the question is generally assumed to be clear enough to make ultimately possible a Yes or a No answer. But the truth is on the contrary that the question is ambiguous in several crucial respects, and hence that no answer to it not itself equally ambiguous can be given until the several senses in which the question may be taken have been distinguished.

2. SURVIVAL FOR HOW LONG AND OF JUST WHAT

Let us agree first that the question in view is not that of "immortality of the soul," but the less ambitious one of discarnate survival of the psychological constituents of the human personality. The two questions are distinct, for on the one hand the notion of "soul" is an elusive theological one, whereas the human mind is observable and analyzable; and on the other "immortality" means incapacity to die and hence life forever, whereas we are concerned only with survival at all, no matter whether for a long or a short or an endless time after death.

The other question—as to just what might survive—has in view first of all the fact that the human personality has bodily constituents as well as psychological ones. The former—the body's features, gait, build, carriage, voice, etc.—are certainly destroyed by the biological disintegration which begins at death. Because of this I shall in what follows speak of survival not of the human personality but only of the human *mind*—using this term to designate the personality's various psychological constituents together.

But the human mind too is a complex. It analyzes into organized sets of "dispositions," that is, of *capacities,* some of them cognitive, others impulsive, and others emotional. That a person is *irritable,* for example, means that if, under ordinary circumstances, something occurs that interferes with his purposes, this causes in him the feeling called anger or irritation; or again, that a person *knows* who was the first president of the Society for Psychical Research means that if, under ordinary circumstances, this question presents itself to him, this causes the name of Henry Sidgwick to come to his mind. And so on. The totality of these interconnected capacities constitutes the *nature* of his mind at a given time, as distinguished from the *history* of his mind up to that time. The history of it, on the other hand, consists of the series of *exercises* of various of its capacities since the time of birth. Items of its history would therefore be, for instance, that on a particular occasion the person concerned did actually become irritated; or did actually recall that Sidgwick was the first president, etc.

Within the mind as consisting of a set of systematically inter-related capacities, however, various sub-systems can be distinguished, some of which might survive and others might not. For example, the capacity to recall past experiences might survive, but perhaps not also the capacity for intellectual initiative and critical judgment. Indeed, survival of the former but not of the latter is what the majority of mediumistic communications would seem to testify to when they suggest at all that something has survived.

3. POSSIBLE KINDS OF "LIFE" AFTER DEATH

Another ambiguity in the question of life after death resides in the word "life" which, of course, cannot be meant in its biological sense after the body has died and the "life," if any, of the mind is then what the question concerns.

(a) The first *prima facie* possibility is that the capacities which together constitute the mind might all persist after death in the same wholly dormant condition as that in which, for instance, one's capacity to perform arithmetical operations persists during periods when one is not performing any.

Use of the word "dormant" to characterize that condition suggests, however, that it is similar to that of the body of a man in

[47]

deep sleep; but if so, note must then be taken of the fact that the body would not be living at all but would be dead unless, even in deep sleep, it were exercising *some* of its capacities; for instance, among others, its capacities to breathe and to circulate its blood. If exercise of these ceased, it could not be resumed, nor could that of any of its dormant higher ones. Indeed, if even the capacities which the dead body shares with the living body—for instance, being visible, tangible, having weight, etc.—ceased to be exercised, then the body would not merely have died: it would have ceased to exist altogether.

But now, since the mind is, like the body, a complex of capacities, the facts just noted suggest that, similarly in the case of the mind, its being *alive at all*—or indeed, existence at all even of what, if anything, could be called the "corpse" of a mind that had died—consists in *actual exercise* of some, anyway, of the mind's capacities; and that, if exercise even of its "vegetative" capacities once ceased, then the mind would be dead and neither the vegetative nor any of the higher capacities it had possessed could ever again be exercised. Thus, complete latency of *all* the mind's capacities would not be a form of mental life at all, nor could it even be persistence of any of the capacities of a mind.

Professor Broad, however, states that we commonly take for granted that "at the back of any . . . purely conditional fact" (such as a disposition or capacity constitutes) there must be "a *categorical* fact of a certain kind, viz., one about the more or less persistent *minute structure* of the thing in question, or about some more or less persistent *recurrent process* going on within it."[3]

But the words "at the back of" are figurative, and so are the words "grounded on" as occurring in the statement that "every conditional fact must be grounded on a categorical fact" (p. 21). And persistence of a minute structure, or of a recurrent process, itself ultimately analyzes as *persistent exercise* of certain capacities. Hence persistence of the psi-component which Professor Broad postulates as persistent "ground" of a mind's capacities can consist only of persistent *exercise* of some (then indeed fundamental) capacities.

---

[3] *Personal Identity and Survival*, the 1958 Myers Memorial Lecture, S.P.R., London, p. 17; also *Human Personality and the Possibility of its Survival*, the 1954 Foerster Lecture, University of California Press, pp. 20, 21.

(b) If a mind's being living at all consists in exercise of at least its "vegetative" capacities, then the next question is, which ones of its capacities does that term designate? The most plausible mental analogues of such bodily activities as breathing and heart-beat would seem to be the mind's automatic, uncensored, and unsought generation of mental images, impulses, and feelings, by one another—an image, for example, spontaneously generating an emotion, and the latter in turn an impulse; or again, a feeling spontaneously generating images and desires kin to it, etc.

But exercise, thus without intent and without criticism, of these wholly internal mental capacities is the kind of mental activity termed *dreaming* or *idle reverie*; and mental life after death might consist of this and nothing more.

(c) A second possible form of mental life after death, less automatic than the above but still wholly subjective, would consist of *reviewing in memory the experiences and activities* of one's *ante mortem* life, attempting as one did so to discern such causal connections as there had been between earlier and later ones; and seeking in this way to harvest what wisdom was latent in them, which at the time one had been too engrossed to garner.

(d) Still another possibility would be that of *post mortem* life consisting of *purposeful and intelligently controlled creative thought*. This would be "living" after death in the sense in which a mathematician, a musical composer, a poet, or a philosopher, etc., is living even before death, when, at times of bodily inactivity and of abstraction from sense stimuli, he is absorbed in wholly mental creative activity.

(e) But a fourth possible form of discarnate life would consist of, or rather include also, *response*—then necessarily telepathic or clairvoyant—to stimuli from a then non-physical environment; and also *action*—then necessarily psychic—upon the excarnate personalities, or the possible impersonal psychic objects, making up that non-physical environment.

A *post mortem* life that would thus include, besides the three kinds of mental activity mentioned before, also interaction of the surviving mind with a non-physical environment, would be the fullest kind of discarnate life, and is what I shall in the sequel mean by discarnate life "in the fullest sense." It is doubtless what the words

[49]

"life after death" are tacitly assumed by most persons to mean; but, as Professor Broad has pointedly remarked, there is no reason to expect that life after death, if any, should be of the same form for all persons.[4]

At this point, we shall say nothing of the possibility of life after death as immediate reincarnation.

4. WHERE EVIDENCE OF SURVIVAL, IF ANY, MIGHT BE FOUND

Several possible meanings of the words "discarnate life after death" having now been distinguished, we come to the question as to where, if survival in one or another of the senses described is a fact, empirical evidence of it might be found.

Obviously, it is not found either in any facts of common experience or in any of the recondite facts brought to light by the physical, the biological, or the social sciences; for otherwise survival would no longer be in doubt. Hence the evidence, if any, of survival must be sought among the rare and paradoxical occurrences termed "supernatural" by naive persons but today designated simply as "paranormal" by persons too critical to assume as the former tacitly do that Nature can comprise only what is known and understood as of now.

The paranormal is simply that which happens to clash with what we have come to regard as normal; that is, with what the "scientific commonsense of the epoch" regards as possible. The physicist, W. F. G. Swann, has pointed out that each theory of the world or of man that is successful enough in accounting for the facts it concerns to gain wide acceptance "grows around itself an aura of commonsense, the commonsense of its epoch." As novel facts are taken into account, however, more adequate theories supersede the old, and "the nonsense of the past becomes the commonsense of the future."[5]

Only certain kinds of ostensibly paranormal occurrences, however, lend themselves to interpretation as *prima facie* evidence of survival. The chief of these would be apparitions, "out-of-the-body" experiences, "possessions," and communications purportedly from the

---

[4] *Human Personality and the Possibility of its Survival, op. cit.,* p. 26.
[5] "Nature and the Mind of Man," *Journal of the Franklin Institute,* Vol. 261, No. 6, June, 1956, p. 593.

surviving deceased obtained through mediums or automatists. Notable among the latter are the communications which have been termed "cross correspondences."

5. QUESTIONS RELEVANT TO REPORTS OF OSTENSIBLY PARANORMAL OCCURRENCES

Certain questions arise at the outset in connection with reports of paranormal occurrences of the above kinds as well as of others; and those questions have in each case to be satisfactorily answered before one is warranted in accepting the occurrence concerned as really paranormal.

Some of the questions concern the *report* itself: Is it objective, or does it consist in part of inferences from the objective facts? Is it detailed, or only general, precise or vague, made from notes taken at the time, or from memory how long after? Other questions concern the *reporter*: Is he truthful, or perhaps mendacious? Impartial, or biased? And still other questions relate to the *observer*: was he competent to observe reliably, under the conditions that existed, what he believed he observed; or was he naively credulous—or indeed, perhaps naively incredulous? If the answers to these questions indicate that the occurrence was really not just seemingly paranormal, then but only then does the question arise as to whether the occurrence affords evidence of survival at all; and if so, then survival of *which constituents* of *whose personality*. For the purposes of the discussion to follow, it will be assumed that some genuinely paranormal cases exist of the kinds of occurrences mentioned, and that the question at issue is then only whether they prove or make probable that survival is a fact.

6. APPARITIONS

Of the various kinds of paranormal occurrences that suggest survival, probably the most impressive to those who experience them are the ones commonly called *apparitions of the dead*. To say that they are hallucinations is probably true in many of the cases, but this does not in itself account for their occurrence; for a hallucination is simply a mental image which has sensory vividness but is not due to stimulation of the senses by a physical object such as would cause similar sensations.

One theory of apparitions is that they are products of the sub-conscious internal workings of the percipient's mind. This, however, would not by itself account for cases where the apparition contains veridical details of which the percipient never had any knowledge as, for instance, in the famous case of the apparition of a girl to her brother nine years after her death, her face bearing a scratch which her mother had accidentally made while preparing the body for burial and had immediately obliterated with powder, never mentioning that distressing fact to anybody.[6]

Nor would the hypothesis of subjectively induced hallucination plausibly account for apparitions repeatedly perceived by several persons together—these persons sometimes numbering up to forty—as in the case of the numerous apparitions of the deceased wife of a Captain Butler near Machiasport in Maine at the beginning of the last century.[7]

The somewhat different supposition that an apparition is a hallucination telepathically induced in the percipient by some *living* person would not account, for instance, for the Chaffin Will case[8]—where the existence and location of a father's will was communicated to a son by the father's apparition four years after his death—unless one postulated (and this without independent evidence of the possibility of it) that a telepathic message can be delayed in transmission for years, or that telepathically received information can remain for several years latent in the recipient's mind.

Anyway, the occurrence of apparitions of the living, as well as of the dead and dying, proves that an apparition is not necessarily evidence that the person perceived has died. But the fact that apparitions of the deceased generally have the same characteristics as apparitions of the living suggests that both are, not subjective hallucinations, but genuine perceptions of something objective. This might be, as some have maintained, a subtle "etheric double" of the physical body of the person concerned; that is, a counterpart of the latter,

---

[6] *Proc.* S.P.R., Vol. 6, 1889-1890, pp. 17-20.

[7] *Immortality Proved by the Testimony of Sense,* by the Rev. A. Cummings, Bath, Maine, 1826. A summary of this case, more readable as well as more accessible than the Rev. Cummings' now rare pamphlet, may be found in William Oliver Stevens' *Unbidden Guests,* Dodd, Mead & Company, N. Y., 1945, pp. 261-269.

[8] *Proc.* S.P.R., Vol. 36, 1926-28, pp. 517-524.

composed of matter of a non-physical, finer kind, and normally interpenetrating the body; but which under special circumstances gets detached from it temporarily during life and permanently at death, and then is the surviving mind's sole vehicle. This hypothesis, however, does not by itself account for the clothing and other accouterments worn by apparitions.

But the apparition might instead be an incomplete materialization of an externalized image of the person concerned originally formed either by himself or by some other person, which like a mist would be visible but not tangible and would naturally include an image also of the person's clothing.[9] A complete materialization could be the same thing, except that it would be tangible as well as visible, and perhaps also audible.

An apparition, however, or even a complete materialization of the likeness of a deceased person would not, *merely as such,* be evidence that the mind of the deceased person concerned continues to *live* either in the full or in one or another of the inferior manners described in Section 3. In order to show that it so continues, an apparition or materialization would have not merely to occur, but to give us the same sorts of evidence of mental life as do the living persons whom we meet every day. And, that the mind of whose life we would then have evidence is *the same* as that of the person the apparition resembles would have to be established by the same kinds of evidence—for instance by its demonstrating possession of memories of the life of that person—which we would use in ascertaining now that a man we speak with is one we used to know, and not perhaps his identical twin whom we never met.

Thus, what would testify, if at all, to mental life's continuation after death and to the identity of the surviving mind would be, as Richet pointed out, *those evidences themselves* and not the fact that they came through an apparition or materialization rather than, perhaps, through the communications of an entranced medium or of an automatic writer.[10]

---

[9] For references to these and to other theories of the nature of apparitions, see "Six Theories about Apparitions," by Hornell Hart, *Proc.* S.P.R., Vol. 50, 1956, pp. 153-239.

[10] *Thirty Years of Psychical Research,* Macmillan Company, New York, 1923, p. 490.

7. "OUT-OF-THE-BODY" EXPERIENCES

The hypothesis that apparitions are perceptions of the somehow momentarily visible "etheric double" of a deceased or of a living person gains support from some of the so-called "out-of-the-body" (or "projection," or "travelling clairvoyance") experiences—those, namely, where the person who has the experience not only finds himself able to observe his sleeping body from a position in space external to it, to travel away from it to distant places, and to observe what is occurring there, but in addition *is seen there* by the persons present. A famous case of such "bilocation" is that of Alfonso de Liguori who in 1774 was in prison at Arezzo, fasting; who, on awakening one morning, stated that he had been at the bedside of the then dying Pope Clement XIV; and who, it turned out, had been seen among those present there.[11]

Persons who have this "projection" experience are wont to interpret it as did a friend of Bozzano's, the engineer Giuseppe Costa, who, after relating an impressive such experience of his, stated: "I had, in fact, received proof of the existence of the soul and also of its immortality, since it was true that it had freed itself . . . from the material envelope of the body, acting and thinking outside it.[12] But of course, separation, *in spatial location,* of the observing consciousness and the living body does not prove that the consciousness is not even then dependent on the *life* of the body. For the so-called "silver cord," which we are told connects the two during their externalization, may not be, as tacitly assumed, a channel through which the spatially detached living "soul *animates* the sleeping body; but may be on the contrary a channel through which the life of the body supports the consciousness which observes it from a point in space external to it (as, essentially, could an eye which, instead of being sunken in the head, were connected with it by a long stalk); so that when the bodily support dies, so would the externally observing consciousness. Hence, "out-of-the-body" experiences do not in themselves constitute evidence of survival of the mind after death.

The cases where the externalized "etheric double" is seen by others suggest, however, that what is seen in the case of apparitions of

---

[11] Richet, *op. cit.,* p. 552.

[12] Quoted in Bozzano's *Discarnate Influence in Human Life,* John M. Watkins, London, 1938, pp. 112-115, from Costa's *Di là della Vita,* p. 18.

the likeness of a deceased person may be his then finally detached but still persisting "etheric double." Whether the mind which was connected with it during life does itself still live, or whether the persisting "etheric double" is then but a mindless "etheric" automaton, is another question, which is not answered by the mere occurrence of the apparition.

8. "POSSESSIONS"

These are cases of *prima facie* possession and use of the body of a given living person by a personality distinct from his own, which, for the time being, disappears. In most cases, the invading personality is probably a dissociated part, until then more or less repressed, of the normal personality. The case of Miss Beauchamp, described by Dr. Morton Prince, and that of Doris Fischer, described by Dr. Walter F. Prince, are famous instances.[13] This hypothesis, however, does not fit the few cases where the "possessing" personality gives abundant evidence of being that of some particular deceased person and where its ability to give that evidence cannot plausibly be accounted for otherwise than by its being what it purports to be. An outstanding case of this is that of the so-called "Watseka Wonder," in which two girls were concerned. One, Mary Roff, living in Watseka, Ill., had died in 1865 at the age of eighteen. The other, Lurancy Vennum, was then fourteen months old, and did not come to Watseka until the age of seven. The acquaintance between her parents and that of the deceased Mary consisted of but a call of a few minutes by Mrs. Roff on Mrs. Vennum and of a formal speaking acquaintance between the two men. At the age of fourteen, Lurancy's personality was displaced by one claiming to be Mary Roff, which did not know the Vennums and asked to go to her parents, who lived some distance away. She was taken to them and there knew every person and every thing that Mary had known in her original body, recognizing and calling by name those who were friends and neighbors of the family during the twelve years which had preceded Lurancy's birth, and giving many other evidences of her identity. Mary's apparent reincarnation in Lurancy's body lasted 3 months

---

[13] *The Dissociation of a Personality,* by Morton Prince, Longmans, Green and Co., New York, 1905; *The Doris Case of Multiple Personality,* by W. F. Prince, *Proc.* A.S.P.R., Vols. 9 and 10, 1915 and 1916.

and 10 days. Then Lurancy's own personality returned to her body and she went back to the Vennums.[14]

William James cites this case, saying that it is "perhaps as extreme a case of 'possession' of the modern sort as one can find." However, he makes no attempt to explain it either as one of dissociated personality, which would hardly seem possible, or otherwise.[15]

9. MEDIUMISTIC COMMUNICATIONS

The communications received through mediums, purportedly from the surviving minds or "spirits" of deceased persons, are too familiar to need describing on the present occasion. Among the most famous and *prima facie* most evidential are some of those given by the late Mrs. Leonore Piper of Boston, who was carefully supervised and systematically studied there and in England by the S.P.R. for some seventeen years.

Professor James H. Hyslop, in commenting on the evidentiality of the communications he had received through her, laid stress not only on the correctness of the information contained in them, but also and especially on the "dramatic interplay of different personalities, the personal traits of the communicator, the emotional tone that was natural to the same, the proper appreciation of a situation or a question, and the unity of consciousness displayed throughout."[16] And Dr. Richard Hodgson, who managed Mrs. Piper's séances for many years, similarly emphasizes, in the case of the communications that purported to emanate from his deceased friend George Pelham, the convincingness of such features as the "swift appreciation of any references to friends of G. P." and the " 'give-and-take' in little incidental conversations" between himself and the G. P. communicator.[17]

But whatever may be the true explanation of these communications, it must allow in some way for the fact that more or less similar communications have been received also from characters out

---

[14] *The Watseka Wonder,* by E. W. Stevens, Religio-Philosophical Publishing House, Chicago, 1887.

[15] *Principles of Psychology,* Henry Holt and Company, New York, 1905, Vol. 1, pp. 396-397.

[16] *Proc.* S.P.R., Vol. 16, 1901, p. 293.

[17] *Proc.* S.P.R., Vol. 13, 1897-1898, p. 328.

of fiction, such as Adam Bede and the Lion of Androcles; and, by Professor G. Stanley Hall, from an imaginary niece of his, Bessie Beals, invented by him especially for the purpose of a séance with Mrs. Piper.

Moreover, communications *prima facie* convincing have been received also from purportedly deceased persons who in fact were living at the time. For example, the peculiar fastidious accent and clear articulation of a voice which addressed Dr. S. G. Soal through the vocal organs of a medium, Mrs. Blanche Cooper, was definitely recognized by him as that of a former schoolmate of his, Gordon Davis, whom he believed to be deceased, and whose statements on that occasion indicated that he believed himself to have died. Yet, at the time, he was living and going about his affairs.[18]

The hypothesis of deceitful spirits, sometimes advanced to account for such cases, would be acceptable for this only if the existence of any discarnate spirits at all had independently been already established.

10. CROSS CORRESPONDENCES

This term refers to a set of automatic scripts dating from the early years of the present century, which purport to emanate from the discarnate minds chiefly of Myers, Gurney, and Sidgwick, but also of Verrall and Butcher. The peculiarity of these scripts lies in the fact that particular ones "correspond" to particular others in a manner analogous to that in which one piece of a jigsaw puzzle corresponds to another: a script by Mrs. Verrall in England, for instance, which made no sense, and another, which also made no sense, written by Mrs. Holland in India without any contact between the two automatists, turned out to make clear sense when the two were combined. And it should be added that, in most of the "cross-correspondence" scripts, the hidden common topic consists not of anything commonplace such as, with a little ingenuity, could be read into almost any two passages from different books, but of some recondite anecdote in the Greek or Latin classics.

These scripts are of outstanding importance in connection with the matter of survival evidence, for two reasons. One is that they

---

[18] *Proc.* S.P.R., Vol. 35, 1925, pp. 560-589.

evidently rule out, or anyway strain to the breaking point, the tele-pathy-clairvoyance explanation of the correspondences between their contents. The other is the evidence they constitute that the devisers of the scheme—purportedly the discarnate Myers, Gurney and Sidg-wick—survive not as mere sets of mental habits or memories, but as still retaining intellectual initiative and ingenuity.

In the opinion of some of the most critical, best informed, and closest students of the scripts—Mr. Piddington, Mrs. Sidgwick, Lord Balfour, Mr. Podmore, Sir Oliver Lodge, Miss Alice Johnson—the cross-correspondence scripts constitute the strongest evidence yet ob-tained that the mind of at least some human beings survives the death of the body in the full sense I have defined earlier.

11. THE ALTERNATIVE TO THE SURVIVAL EXPLANATION

The only hypothesis alternative to that of survival that has yet been offered by anyone fully acquainted with all the relevant facts, is that the medium's or automatist's subconscious mind obtains the facts she communicates from the minds of living persons who know them, or from existing documents in which they are recorded, res-pectively, by telepathy or by clairvoyance. This is the contention of, for example, Professor E. R. Dodds in a paper entitled "Why I Do Not Believe in Survival,"[19] where he offers ten criticisms of various grounds that have been advanced for belief in survival and shows that these grounds—or rather, certain ones of them—are adequately dis-posed of by the telepathy-clairvoyance hypothesis.

In order to be in position to evaluate the merits of the telepathy-clairvoyance explanation, however, it is necessary first to state ex-plicitly all that it has to postulate if it is to be adequate to account for all the facts. For one thing, the telepathic or clairvoyant powers ascribed to the medium's subconscious mind have to be virtually limitless. But secondly, the medium's subconscious has to be supposed gifted with an equally extraordinary ability to translate *instantly* the facts it is so learning from various minds into the verisimilar dramatic form her communication of them assumes in the quick give-and-take of conversation with the sitter. And, in addition, one has to postulate that the medium's subconscious telepathic or clairvoyant powers do

---

[19] *Proc.* S.P.R., Vol. 42, 1934, pp. 147-172.

not always discriminate (a) between information from the living about the dead, and information from the living about themselves, nor (b) between information from the living about the dead, and information from the living about fictitious characters invented by or familiar to the living.

Needless to say, this elaborate yet minimal alternative hypothesis will, to many persons, seem more implausible than that of survival.

As regards the cross correspondences, Professor Dodds acknowledges that they manifest pattern, but holds that it is not necessarily due to design; and he agrees anyway with the suggestion others had made that Mrs. Verrall's subconscious mind could well be supposed to have devised the whole scheme.

But then, much more than subconscious invention of it by her and "telepathic leakage" from her mind to those of the other automatists would have to be supposed, namely, *unconscious virtual dictation telepathically* by her of the scripts of the other automatists—this *ad hoc* supposition going, of course, far beyond anything independently known as to what telepathy can do. To ascribe their scripts simply to telepathic leakage from her mind will hardly suffice, for as Lord Balfour remarked concerning such a proposal by Miss F. M. Stawell in the "Ear of Dionysius" case "it is not at all clear how 'telepathic leakage' could be so thoughtful as to arrange all the topics in such an ingenious way. It seems a little like 'explaining' the working of a motor car by saying that it goes because petrol leaks out of a tank into the front end!"[20]

12. WHAT EVIDENCE WOULD PROVE SURVIVAL, AND HOW THE QUESTION NOW STANDS

The difficult task of deciding where the various kinds of facts now before us, the rival interpretations of them, and the criticisms of the interpretations, finally leave the case for the reality of survival requires that we first attempt to specify what evidence, if we should have it, we would accept as definitely proving survival or, short of this, as definitely establishing a positive probability that survival is a fact.

To this end, let us suppose that a friend of ours, John Doe, was

---

[20] *Proc.* S.P.R., Vol. 29, 1916-1918, p. 270.

a passenger on the transatlantic plane which some months ago the newspapers reported crashed shortly after leaving Shannon without having radioed that it was in trouble. Since no survivors were reported to have been found, we would natually assume that John Doe had died with the others. Let us now, however, consider in turn each of three further suppositions:

(a) The first is that some time later we meet on the street a man we recognize as John Doe, who recognizes us too, and who has John Doe's voice and mannerisms. Also, that allusions to personal matters familiar to both of us, made now in our conversation with him, are readily understood and suitably responded to by each. Then, even before he tells us how he chanced to survive the crash, we would of course *know* that, somehow, he has survived it.

(b) But now, let us suppose instead that we do not thus meet him, but that one day our telephone rings and over the line comes a voice which we clearly recognize as John Doe's; and that we also recognize certain turns of phrase that were peculiar to him. He tells us that he survived the disaster, and we then talk with ready mutual understanding about personal and other matters that had been familiar to the two of us. We wish, of course, that we could see him as well as thus talk with him; yet we would feel practically certain that he had survived the crash and is now living.

(c) Let us, however, now consider instead a third supposition, namely, that one day, when our telephone rings, a voice not John Doe's tells us that he did survive the accident and that he wants us to know it, but that for some reason he cannot come to the phone. He is, however, in need of money and wants us to deposit some to his account in the bank.

Then of course—especially since the person who transmits the request over the telephone sounds at times a bit incoherent—we would want to make very sure that the person from whom the request emanates is really John Doe. To this end, we ask him through the intermediary to name some mutual friends; and he names several, giving some particular facts about each. We refer, allusively, to various personal matters he would be familiar with; and it turns out that he understands the allusions and responds to them relevantly. Also, the intermediary quotes him as uttering various statements, in which we recognize peculiarities of his thought and phraseology; and the peculiar nasal tone of his voice is imitated by the intermediary well enough for us to recognize it.

Would all this convince us that the request for money really emanates from John Doe and that he therefore did survive the accident and is still living? If we should react rationally rather than impulsively, our becoming convinced or remaining unconvinced would depend on the following considerations.

First, *is it possible at all* that our friend somehow did survive the crash? If, for example, his dead body had been subsequently found and identified beyond question, then obviously the person whose request for money is being transmitted to us *could not possibly be* John Doe not yet deceased; and hence the identifying evidence conveyed to us over the phone would necessarily be worthless, no matter how strongly it would otherwise testify to his being still alive.

But if we have no such antecedent conclusive proof that he did perish, then the degree of our confidence that the telephoned request ultimately does emanate from him and hence that he is still living will depend for us on the following three factors.

(a) One will be the *abundance,* or *scantiness,* of such evidence of his identity as comes to us over the phone.

(b) A second factor will be the *quality* of the evidence. That is, does it correspond *minutely* and *in peculiar details* to what we know of the facts or incidents to which it refers; or on the contrary does it correspond to them merely in that it gives, correctly indeed, the *broad* features of the events concerned, but *does not include much detail?*

(c) The third factor will be that of *diversity of the kinds of evidence* the telephoned messages supply. Does all the evidence, for example, consist *only of correct memories* of personal matters and of matters typical of John Doe's range of information? Or does the evidence include also *dramatic faithfulness* of the communications to the manner, the attitudes, the tacit assumptions, and the idiosyncrasies of John Doe as we remember him? And again, do the communications manifest in addition something which H. F. Saltmarsh has held to be "as clear an indication of psychical individuality as finger prints are of physical,"[21] namely, *associations of ideas that were peculiar to*

---

[21] *Evidence of Personal Survival from Cross Correspondences,* G. Bell & Sons, London, 1938, p. 34.

John Doe as of the age he had reached at the time of the crash? If these same associations are still manifest, then persistence of them will signify one thing if the communication in which they appear is made not too long after the accident, but a different thing if instead it is made, say, twenty-five years after. For a person's associations of ideas alter more or less as a result of new experiences, of changes of environment, of acquisition of new ranges of information, and of development of new interests. Hence, if the associations of ideas are the same a few months or a year or two after the accident as they were before, this would testify to John Doe's identity. But if they are the same a quarter of a century later, then this would testify rather that although some of the capacities he had have apparently persisted, yet he has in the meantime *not continued really to live;* for to "live" in the full sense of the word entails becoming gradually different—indeed, markedly different in many ways over such a long term of years.

Now, the point of our introducing the case of John Doe, and of the three suppositions we made in succession as to occurrences that convinced us, or that inclined us in various degrees to believe, that he had not after all died in the plane accident is that the second and especially the third of these suppositions duplicate in all essentials the evidences of survival of the human mind which the best of the mediumistic communications supply. For the medium or automatist is the analogue of the telephone and, in cases of apparent possession of the medium's organism by the purported communicator, the latter is the analogue of John Doe when himself telephoning. The medium's "control," on the other hand, is the analogue of the intermediary who at other times transmits John Doe's statements over the telephone. And the fact mentioned at the beginning of this paper—that survival has not been proved to be either empirically or logically impossible—is the analogue of the supposition that John Doe's body was never found and hence that his having survived the crash is not known to be impossible.

This parallelism between the two situations entails that if reason rather than either religious or materialistic faith is to decide, then our answer to the question whether the evidence we have today does or does not establish survival (or at least a positive probability of it) must, in the matter of survival after death, be based on the very same considerations as in the matter of survival after the loss of the plane. That is, our answer will have to be based on the *quantity of evidence* we get over the mediumistic "telephone"; on the *quality* of it in the sense defined; and on the *diversity* of kinds of it we get.

To what conclusion, then, do these three considerations point when brought to bear on the evidence referred to in Sections 6 to 10 above? The conclusion they dictate is, I believe, the same as that which was reached in the end by Mrs. Sidgwick, by Lord Balfour, by Professor Hyslop, by Dr. Hodgson, by Sir Oliver Lodge, and by a number of others—all of them persons who were thoroughly familiar with the evidence on record; who were gifted with keenly critical minds; who had originally been skeptical of the reality or even possibility of survival; and who were also fully acquainted with the evidence for the reality of telepathy and of clairvoyance, and with the claims that had been made for the telepathy-clairvoyance interpretation of the evidence, as against the survival interpretation of it.

Their conclusion was essentially that the balance of the evidence so far obtained is on the side of the reality of survival and, in the best cases, of survival not merely of memories of the life on earth, but of survival also of the most significant capacities of the human mind, and of continuing exercise of them after death.